breeze-easy method

Trombone

by John Kinyon

Cover photo courtesy of C.G. Conn.

FOREWORD

This METHOD is designed to give the young student a proper conception and systematic approach to music reading and the art of brass performance. Emphasis is on the fundamentals including tone production, tone placement, embouchure development, technique, rhythmic perception and tonal consciousness. Through this thorough and efficient course of study the student will be led to take his place as a contributing member of the school band or orchestra in the shortest possible time.

The TRUMPET, TROMBONE and BARITONE books may be used in conjunction with one another, thus facilitating the organization of beginning brass classes. The book also contains a refreshing repertoire of new song material that will delight both student and teacher.

John Kinyon

PLAYING POSITIONS

STUDY THESE PICTURES AND NOTICE THE FOLLOWING IMPORTANT POINTS:

1. GOOD BODY POSTURE.

2. THE LEFT HAND SUPPORTS THE WEIGHT OF THE INSTRUMENT, THE RIGHT HAND IS RELAXED.

3. THE INSTRUMENT SLANTS SLIGHTLY DOWNWARD TO CONFORM WITH THE NATURAL ANGLE OF THE JAW.

4. THE MOUTHPIECE IS IN THE CENTER OF THE LIP; THE MUSCLES AT THE CORNERS OF THE MOUTH ARE FIRM, BUT CONTROLLED.

5. THE CHEEKS ARE NOT PUFFED OUT.

PRELIMINARY LESSON

THINGS YOU SHOULD KNOW BEFORE WE BEGIN:

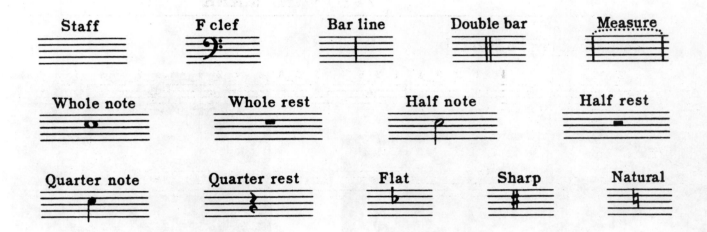

Staff   F clef   Bar line   Double bar   Measure

Whole note   Whole rest   Half note   Half rest

Quarter note   Quarter rest   Flat   Sharp   Natural

TIME SIGNATURES

$\frac{4}{4}$ means four counts in each measure $\frac{3}{4}$ means three counts in each measure $\frac{2}{4}$ means two counts in each measure

NAMES OF NOTES

G A B C D E F G A

DO NOT PUFF OUT YOUR CHEEKS!

OUR FIRST TONES

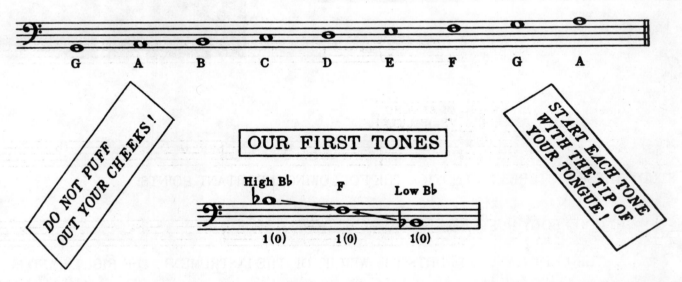

High B♭   F   Low B♭

1(0)   1(0)   1(0)

START EACH TONE WITH THE TIP OF YOUR TONGUE!

YOUR TEACHER WILL SHOW YOU HOW TO PLAY CORRECTLY. ONE OF THE ABOVE THREE TONES WILL COME EASIER FOR YOU THAN THE OTHERS. YOUR TEACHER WILL TELL YOU WHICH ONE YOU ARE PLAYING. PRACTICE HOLDING THIS TONE FOR SEVERAL COUNTS UNTIL YOU GET THE FEEL OF IT. NOW YOU MUST TRY TO PLAY THE TONE F. *IF THE HIGH B♭ COMES EASIEST FOR YOU*, YOU MUST RELAX THE CORNERS OF YOUR LIP SLIGHTLY IN ORDER TO PRODUCE THE LOWER PITCH; *IF THE LOW B♭ COMES EASIEST FOR YOU*, YOU MUST TIGHTEN THE CORNERS SLIGHTLY IN ORDER TO PRODUCE THE HIGHER PITCH. WHEN YOU CAN PLAY THE F WITH A FULL TONE AND IN A RELAXED MANNER, YOU ARE READY TO PROCEED WITH LESSON ONE.

(All New Notes and Material will be placed in a box at the beginning of each lesson.)

LESSON 1.

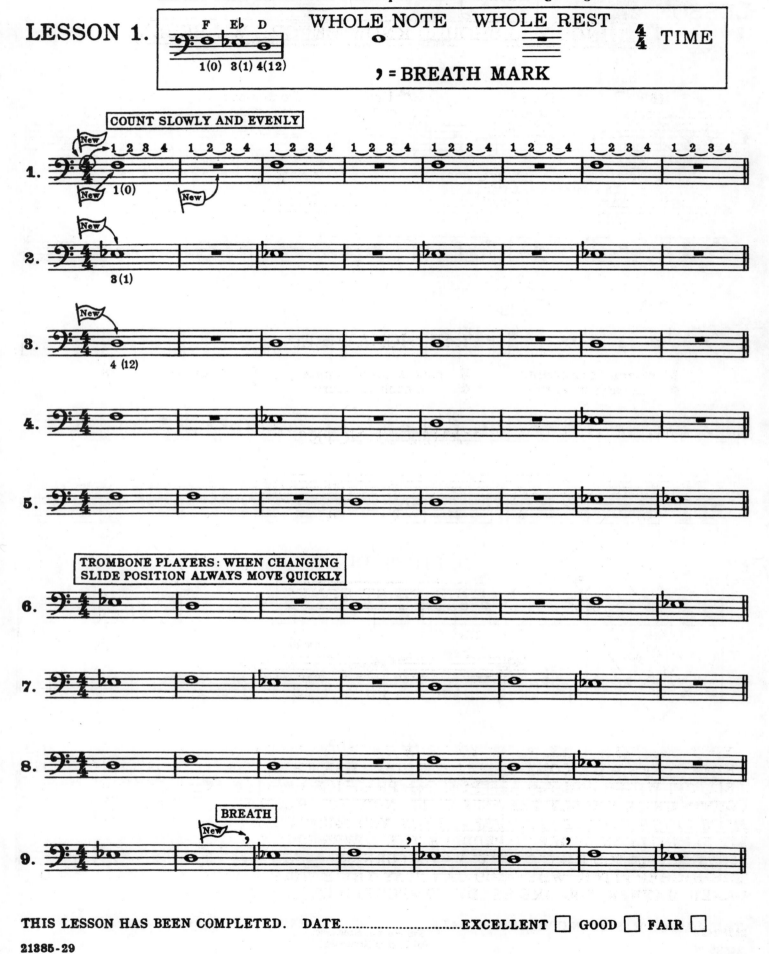

THIS LESSON HAS BEEN COMPLETED.   DATE.............................EXCELLENT ☐ GOOD ☐ FAIR ☐

LESSON 2.

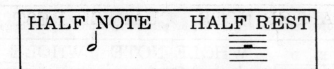

THIS LESSON HAS BEEN COMPLETED. DATE..................................... EXCELLENT ☐ GOOD ☐ FAIR ☐

21385-29

LESSON 3.

| QUARTER NOTE | QUARTER REST | 2/4 TIME |

THIS LESSON HAS BEEN COMPLETED. DATE.................... EXCELLENT ☐ GOOD ☐ FAIR ☐

21385-29

8

LESSON 4.

TISKET-A-TASKET

Go quickly to next line.

COPY CATS

J.K.

THIS LESSON HAS BEEN COMPLETED. DATE........................EXCELLENT ☐ GOOD ☐ FAIR ☐

21385-29

LESSON 5.

DOTTED HALF NOTE 𝅗𝅥. ¾ TIME

LOO-BY-LOO

Traditional

WALTZ DUET

J.K.

THIS LESSON HAS BEEN COMPLETED. DATE........................ EXCELLENT ☐ GOOD ☐ FAIR ☐

21385-29

LESSON 6.

NEW TONE   THE TIE

POP GOES THE WEASEL

Traditional

LONDON BRIDGE

Traditional

* Trombone players ask your
teacher about an easier way
to play this.

THIS LESSON HAS BEEN COMPLETED. DATE................EXCELLENT ☐ GOOD ☐ FAIR ☐

21385-29

LESSON 7.

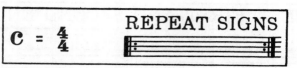

C = 4/4   REPEAT SIGNS

LOVELY EVENING

This may be played as a round.
Ask your teacher how it works.

Traditional Round

2 + 2 = 4

J.K

THIS LESSON HAS BEEN COMPLETED.   DATE.................................EXCELLENT ☐ GOOD ☐ FAIR ☐

21385-29

LESSON 8.

OLD MACDONALD

Traditional

MIXUP

Upon completion of this lesson the student will find much enjoyment in playing from BREEZE-EASY RECITAL PIECES—Book I by JOHN KINYON. This collection of well-known songs has been arranged in the simplest possible fashion and is available with piano accompaniment.

THIS LESSON HAS BEEN COMPLETED. DATE .... EXCELLENT ☐ GOOD ☐ FAIR ☐

LESSON 9.

THE SLUR

* CONNECT THESE TWO TONES

New

1.

CONNECT THESE THREE TONES

2.

CONNECT THESE FIVE TONES

3.

4.

5.

LITTLE ETUDE

J.K.

6.

LIP BUILDER

7.

Trombone players have an easier way to play these two measures.

PENNY AND JENNY

J.K.

8.

* Trombone players have a special problem with slurs. Have your teacher explain this.

THIS LESSON HAS BEEN COMPLETED. DATE.................................EXCELLENT ☐ GOOD ☐ FAIR ☐

21385-29

14

LESSON 10.

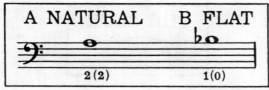

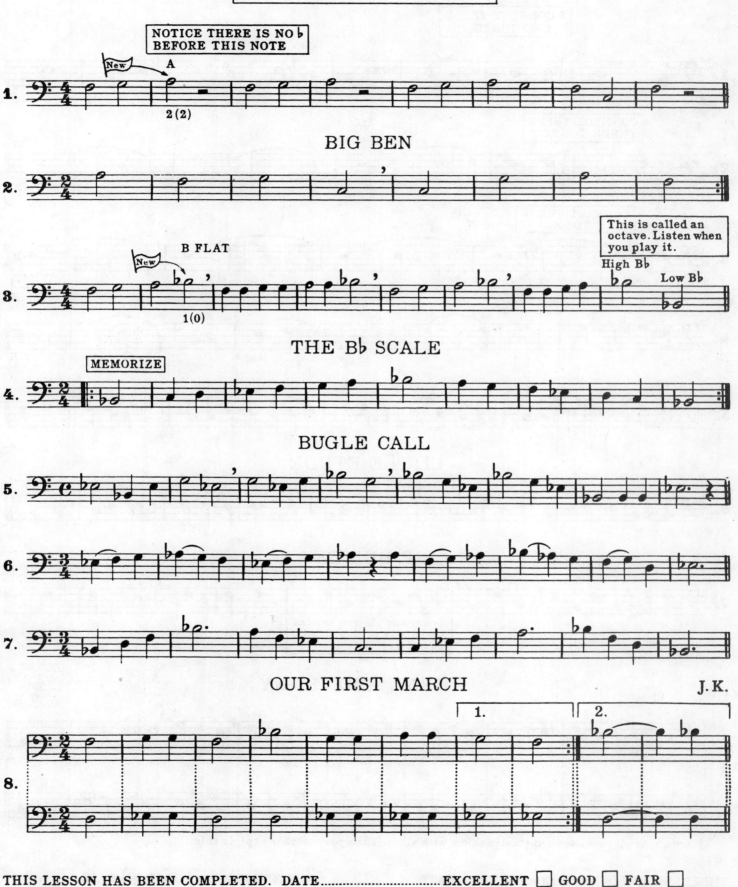

THIS LESSON HAS BEEN COMPLETED. DATE................EXCELLENT ☐ GOOD ☐ FAIR ☐
21385-29

LESSON 11.

PICK-UP NOTES	*p* = SOFT	KEY OF B FLAT
	f = LOUD	
		ALL B's AND E's ARE FLAT

RED RIVER VALLEY — Cowboy Song

BILLY BOY — Traditional

THE TWO FLATS IN THE BEGINNING MEAN ALL B's AND E's ARE FLAT. THIS IS CALLED THE KEY OF B FLAT.

( ) = JUST A REMINDER

AN ARMY MARCH — GRUBER

NOTICE THE KEY SIGNATURE

THIS LESSON HAS BEEN COMPLETED. DATE.................EXCELLENT ☐ GOOD ☐ FAIR ☐

21385-29

LESSON 12.

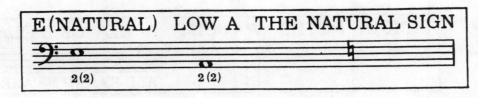

E (NATURAL) LOW A THE NATURAL SIGN

CHROMATIC CAPERS

J.K.

THIS CANCELS THE E♭ FOR THE REST OF THE MEASURE

THESE ARE CALLED LIP SLURS. DO NOT TONGUE THE SECOND TONE OF THE SLUR.

CAN YOU PLAY THIS WITH YOUR EYES CLOSED?

p-f (First time soft, second time loud)

THE CARNIVAL OF VENICE

Folk Song

WHAT KEY IS THIS?

THIS LESSON HAS BEEN COMPLETED. DATE..................................EXCELLENT ☐ GOOD ☐ FAIR ☐

LESSON 13.

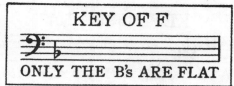

KEY OF F

ONLY THE B's ARE FLAT

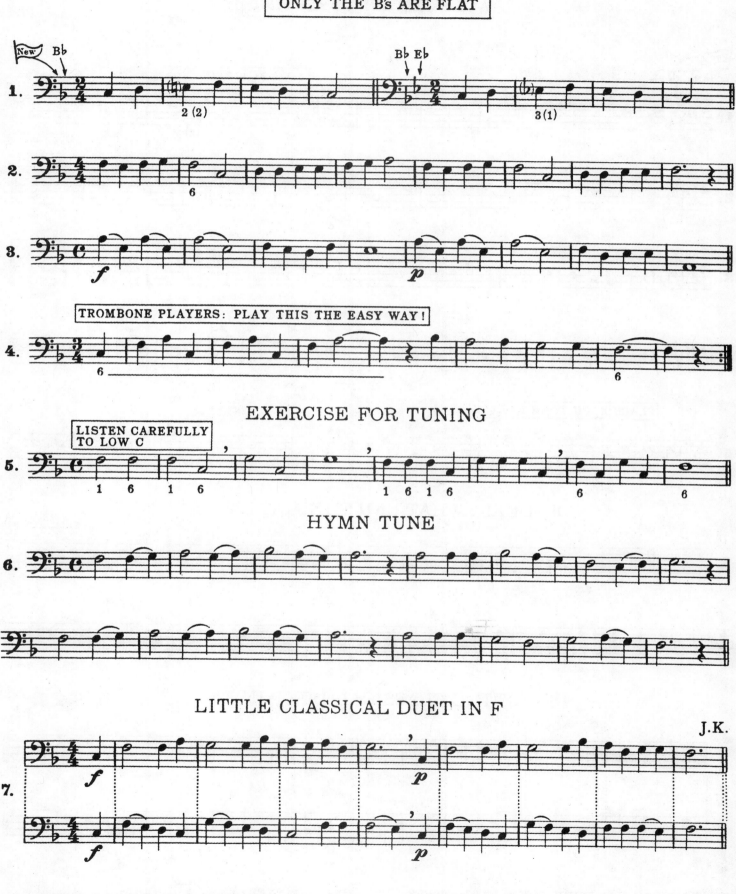

TROMBONE PLAYERS: PLAY THIS THE EASY WAY!

EXERCISE FOR TUNING

LISTEN CAREFULLY TO LOW C

HYMN TUNE

LITTLE CLASSICAL DUET IN F

J.K.

THIS LESSON HAS BEEN COMPLETED. DATE............................ EXCELLENT ☐ GOOD ☐ FAIR ☐

21385-29

LESSON 14.

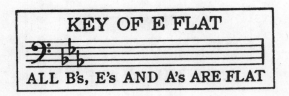

KEY OF E FLAT

ALL B's, E's AND A's ARE FLAT

PLACE EACH TONE NEATLY

OH DEAR, WHAT CAN THE MATTER BE?

Traditional

LITTLE CLASSICAL DUET IN E♭

J. K.

THIS LESSON HAS BEEN COMPLETED. DATE.................................EXCELLENT ☐ GOOD ☐ FAIR ☐

LESSON 15.

MY WILD IRISH ROSE

OLCOTT

THIS LESSON HAS BEEN COMPLETED. DATE................EXCELLENT ☐ GOOD ☐ FAIR ☐

20

LESSON 16.

EIGHTH NOTES *mf* = MEDIUM LOUD
mp = MEDIUM SOFT

THE ERIE CANAL
Traditional

ETUDE IN B♭
J.K.

LITTLE CANON
J.K.

THIS LESSON HAS BEEN COMPLETED. DATE........................EXCELLENT ☐ GOOD ☐ FAIR ☐

21385-29

LESSON 17.

REPEAT SIGN FOR ONE MEASURE
∕.

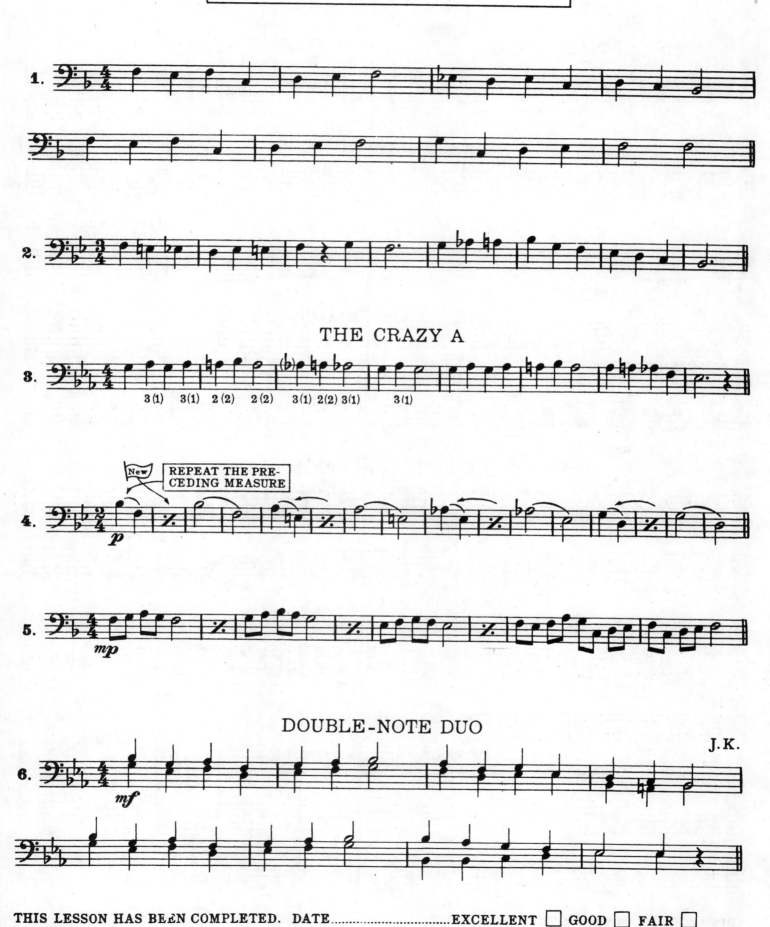

THE CRAZY A

DOUBLE-NOTE DUO

J.K.

THIS LESSON HAS BEEN COMPLETED. DATE...................EXCELLENT ☐ GOOD ☐ FAIR ☐

21385-29

LESSON 18.

22

EIGHTH REST	ACCENT
7	>

FAMILIAR TUNE

HAYDN

FIRST VARIATION

SECOND VARIATION

POLKA DOT POLKA

J.K.

THIS LESSON HAS BEEN COMPLETED. DATE.............................EXCELLENT ☐ GOOD ☐ FAIR ☐

21385-29

LESSON 19.

LOW A FLAT

THIS LESSON HAS BEEN COMPLETED. DATE.................EXCELLENT ☐ GOOD ☐ FAIR ☐

LESSON 21.

THE DOTTED QUARTER AND EIGHTH   THE HOLD   *ritard.* (rit.)

THIS LESSON HAS BEEN COMPLETED.   DATE.................EXCELLENT ☐ GOOD ☐ FAIR ☐

LESSON 22.

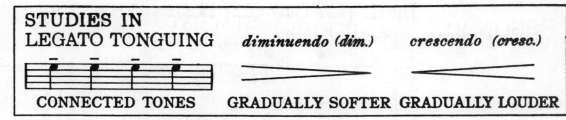

STUDIES IN LEGATO TONGUING	diminuendo (dim.)	crescendo (cresc.)
CONNECTED TONES	GRADUALLY SOFTER	GRADUALLY LOUDER

CONNECT THESE TONES AS CLOSELY AS POSSIBLE

ALL SONGS SHOULD BE PLAYED AS LEGATO AS POSSIBLE

O, NO JOHN

Andante

Traditional

LITTLE SONG

Legato

MOZART

rit.

TAPS

Legato

Bugle Call

dim................

FATHER OF VICTORY MARCH

MARCHES ARE USUALLY PLAYED IN A MORE DETACHED STYLE

GANNE

cresc. - - - - - -

THIS LESSON HAS BEEN COMPLETED. DATE...................................EXCELLENT ☐ GOOD ☐ FAIR ☐

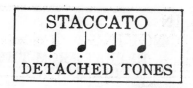

LESSON 23.

STACCATO
DETACHED TONES

27

THEME FROM THE "SURPRISE" SYMPHONY — HAYDN

IN THE HALL OF THE MOUNTAIN KING — GRIEG

JUNIOR HIGH JAMBOREE *(March) — J.K.

TROMBONE-BARITONE

* From the "JOHN KINYON CONCERT BAND FOLIO" (Remick)

THIS LESSON HAS BEEN COMPLETED. DATE.................................EXCELLENT ☐ GOOD ☐ FAIR ☐
21385-29

LESSON 24.

SYNCOPATION	Da Capo D. C.	Dal Segno D. S.	Fine
♪♪ ♪	REPEAT FROM THE BEGINNING	REPEAT FROM THE SIGN (%)	THE END

THESE MEASURES ARE PLAYED THE SAME

1. New

LIZA JANE

Traditional

Allegro

2. *mf staccato*

RUSSIAN SAILOR'S DANCE

Traditional

Allegro

3. *f*

THE RIDDLE SONG

Kentucky Folk Tune

Andante

4. *p legato*

CARRY ME BACK TO OLD VIRGINNY

BLAND

5. *mp legato*

New %   New → Fine

New → D.S. al Fine, %

GO BACK TO THE SIGN (%) AND END AT THE *Fine*

LARGO

DVORAK
Fine

6. *p legato*

New → D.C. al Fine

GO BACK TO THE BEGINNING AND END AT *Fine*

THIS LESSON HAS BEEN COMPLETED. DATE.................... EXCELLENT ☐ GOOD ☐ FAIR ☐

21385-29

LESSON 25.

TROMBONE PLAYERS: LEARN THIS HANDY POSITION FOR B FLAT

TROMBONE PLAYERS: FIGURE OUT THE EASIEST WAY TO PLAY THIS

THUNDER AND BLAZES MARCH

FUCIK

THIS LESSON HAS BEEN COMPLETED. DATE..................**EXCELLENT** ☐ **GOOD** ☐ **FAIR** ☐

21385-29

LESSON 26.

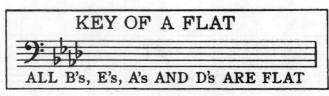

KEY OF A FLAT

ALL B's, E's, A's AND D's ARE FLAT

THE A FLAT SCALE

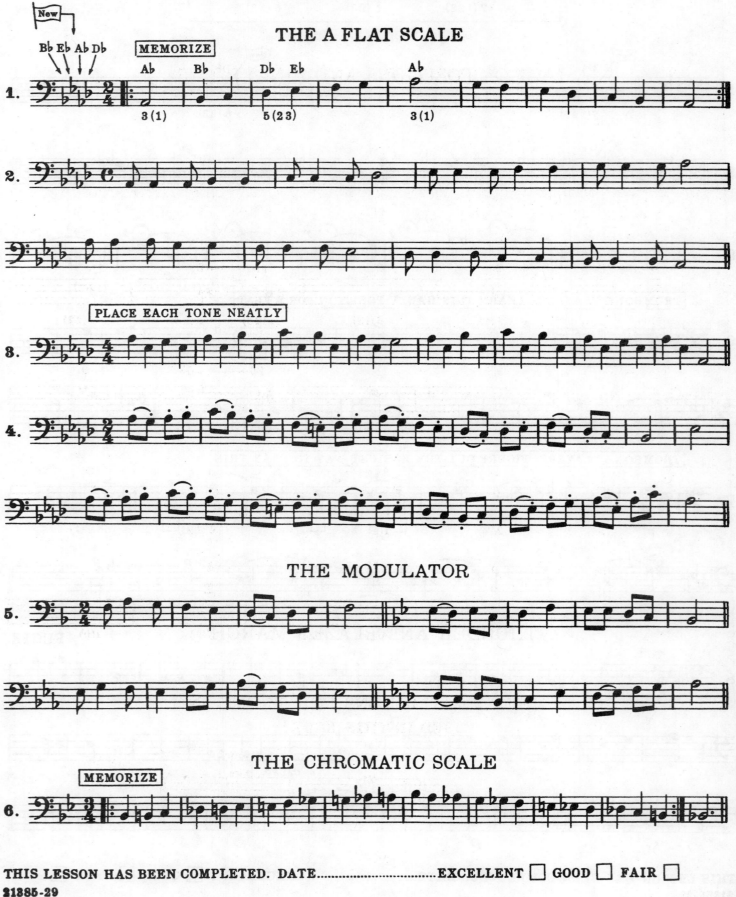

MEMORIZE

PLACE EACH TONE NEATLY

THE MODULATOR

THE CHROMATIC SCALE

MEMORIZE

THIS LESSON HAS BEEN COMPLETED. DATE...................................EXCELLENT ☐ GOOD ☐ FAIR ☐

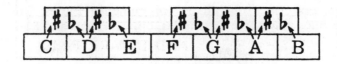

CHART OF POSITIONS AND FINGERINGS

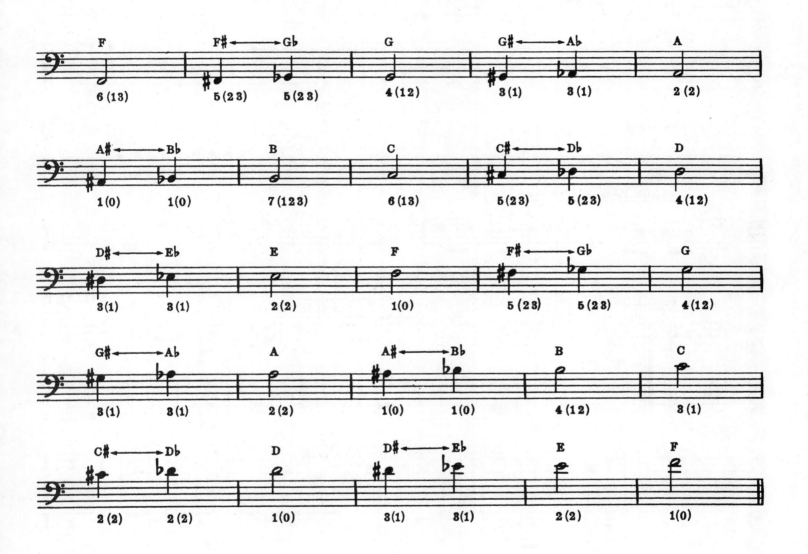

ALTERNATE POSITIONS FOR TROMBONE
(USED IN THIS BOOK)

32

The pieces on this page may be played as Solos, Duets, Trios and Rounds as indicated under each title. These Ensembles may be played by groups of "like" or "mixed" instruments (Flutes, Oboes, Trumpets, Drums, etc. may play together). When "mixed" groups play these Ensembles, only F Horns and Eb Saxophones may be used.